The Adventures of SHIMA the SHIBA

Written by
Mike Missanelli

Illustrated by
Alexander T. Lee

ISBN: 978-1-77883-065-5 (Paperback)

978-1-77883-066-2 (Hardback)

The views expressed in this book are solely those of the author and do not necessarily reflect the views of the publisher, and the publisher hereby disclaims any responsibility for them.

BookSide Press
877-741-8091
www.booksidepress.com
orders@booksidepress.com

The **Adventures** OF

SHIMA THE SHIBA

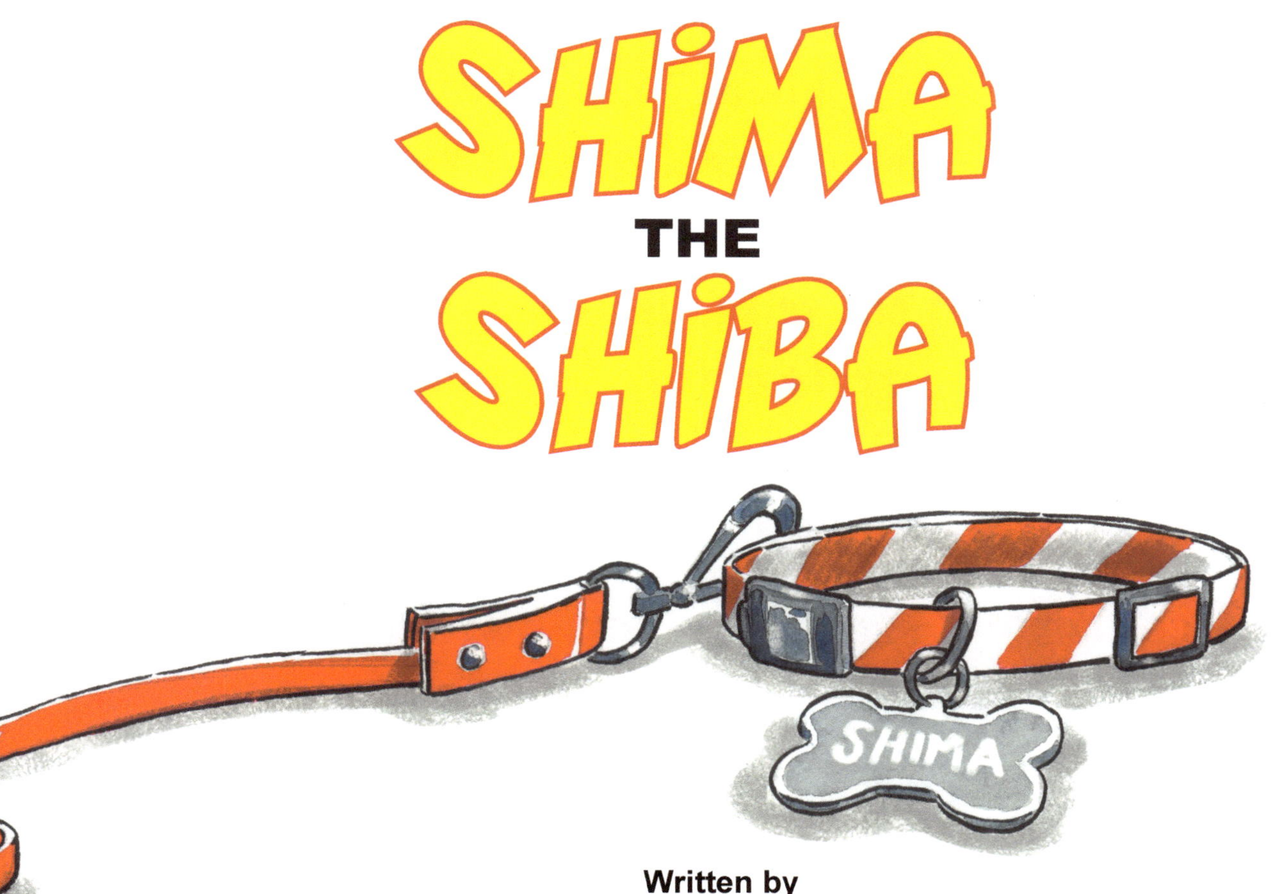

Written by

Mike Missanelli

Illustrated by

Alexander T. Lee

Hi! My name is Shima. I am a breed called a Shiba Inu. My ancestors are from the country of Japan. We were bred there as hunting dogs who like to find and chase small animals such as birds, rabbits and squirrels before they do damage to our owners' yards, especially if they have nice flower or vegetable gardens.

People say I look like a fox. But I'm cuddlier than a fox and I'm a very good family pet.

People also say Shibas are very stubborn dogs. But I just think we are just very independent and freethinking, which is good.

Come with me on an adventure!

I was just a tiny little puppy the day the man I now call my Dad showed up at the shelter. Can you give me a good home?

Bye Guys.

I'm on my way to a new life and I have so many questions.
What kind of home will I have? Will I have a yard to run in?
I am a little scared.

But it is ok to be a little scared about new experiences.
And it is OK to have emotions. My Dad is calling me Shima.
He says it's short for Shimashita, which in Japanese means "regal!"

I have not yet learned right from wrong. Sometimes I go potty in the house.
Sometimes I escape when the front door is open and I run into the neighborhood to explore.
7

That frustrates my dad, but I don't mean any harm. I'm just having puppy fun!

My dad has tried to train me the normal way dogs are trained.
He took me to the large pet store, where I was put in
a class with other dogs.

The trainer tried to teach us the basics,
 like "come" and "sit."

I did it for a while, but then
I got bored. And the pet store
smells funny.

My dad has taken me for my first visit to the veterinarian, which is a doctor for pets. I must get my shots to protect myself from getting sick. There is no reason to be afraid to go to the doctor because she is always trying to make you better!

For now,
it's mayhem play time!

No
Shima!
No!

No
Shima!
No!

Curiosity can get you in trouble. A big dog lives next door to me, on the other side of the backyard fence.

I hear him barking all the time and I wanted to know why. I thought that all dogs were supposed to be friendly, but not this guy. He did not like it when I crawled under the fence and wandered into his yard.

And he bit me! Ouch!

Well, I suffered a bad cut and the Vet had to give me stitches. But the worst part is that I had to wear this goofy plastic hood around my neck for a really long time so I wouldn't lick the stitches so the wound would heal. **I look ridiculous!**

I don't think I'm a very good watchdog. When I hear noises, like when the mailman comes or someone knocks on the door, I bark and my bark sounds like a wolf in the forest. But when my dad answers the door, I'm friendly and bring that person one of my toys.

But my dad explained to me that perhaps not all visitors will be friendly.

Darn,
Shima's out today
and I'm hungry !

I'm on produce patrol. My dad
likes me to guard his vegetables.

I am fascinated by moving
water and I like to eat it!

I love water ... but I HATE taking a bath ... and I do NOT care about smelling good!!

Since I have a backyard to roam, I am not that crazy about walks (I know, that is strange). But when I do go on walks, I like people more than I like other dogs...

Shibas have this thing about territory.

EVERYTIME someone stops to pet me, they say the same thing, every single time. OK ... all together now:

On a walk, I get frustrated when I see a critter and I can't get them!

Oh ... you guys are SO lucky that I am on this leash right now ... !

hmmm...

I spend a lot of time in my backyard.
Sometimes I just like to bathe in the sun.

My favorite thing to do is play baseball! I follow the hops of the ball and snatch it out of the air!

Remember to follow your dreams. You can be anything you wish to be. I want to be the first doggie professional baseball player!

Do not always follow whatever your friends do, if those things are bad! My neighbors, Penelope and Rose are Bassett Hounds that bark like crazy and scare people just walking by!

But it looks like fun, so I then I do it!

I love the beach and digging in the sand.
But why are these waves coming at me?!
What is THIS thing?

I like people food better than dog food! Here's how I get it. I just look embarrassed for asking and humans will give you anything!

All dogs love
crunchy tiny treats.

But sometimes my dad
gives me bigger ones.

They take too much effort to eat.
So I run off and hide them in very
strange places.

After a long day of running and jumping and eating and barking, a Shiba gets very tired, and can't wait to snuggle in bed.

Good night all. See you next time.